Sorcery and Sorcerers

A Classic Article on the History of Black Magic

By

Sax Rohmer

British Library Cataloguing-in-Publication Data
A catalogue record for this book is available from
the British Library

SORCERY AND SORCERERS

I. THE VEIL

TO-DAY is notable for a curious change in Western thought, or, properly, in a phase of Western thought, more appreciable by churchmen, theosophists, and other students of the Unseen than by the laymen. I refer to a growing discontent with, and a falling away from, revealed religion. It is an age of groping; and whereas one who stumbles onward in the mist nearly always strays from the broad highway into the bypaths that lead to the meres, some may strike a fair and narrow road and emerge upon the mountain top.

Of guides to these divers fairways there are many, some of honesty unimpeachable if poor pilots, others masters of their craft but slaves to greed. Apollonius of Tyana was one of the former; Cagliostro, possibly, belonged to the latter class. No man who has proclaimed himself potent to raise the Veil has ever lacked disciples; no man tendering such a claim ever shall, certainly not in this miracle-hungry century.

" What seek ye ? " demands the Adept.

Comes a chorus from poor purblind humanity:

" To bridge the gulf ! "

But over this gulf floats a mist, beyond the mist hangs a Veil. Has any man, braving the mist, ever thrown a bridge, however frail, across to the shadow bank ? Honest weighing of the evidence would certainly make it appear that so much has been accomplished. With what result ? With the result that the intrepid explorer has obtained a closer view of the Veil.

Now, all exploration of this kind unavoidably leads us into the realms of magic. These are extensive, certainly, and offer prospects more startlingly dissimilar, as we look to right or left, than any tract in nature, not excepting the famous Yellowstone Park. And modern occultism has not made more easy the way ; it has accomplished little beyond the coining of a number of new terms. Sorcery, I think, covers them all. Father Henry Day, S.J., speaking at Manchester, advanced a similar opinion, but classed all magic as Black, when he said :

" The Church condemns the new form of modern spiritism as she condemned the old superstitions. They are identical with devil-worship, with black magic, with the necromancy of the past. Whatever may be said of the pretensions of the spiritism of the day, the Church regards it as the continuation of Satan's revolt against God."

His words are characteristic of the unchanging attitude of the Church of Rome towards magical practices ; and, in so far as they warn would-be dabblers to refrain from sorcery, they are of value. The dangers of magic are not chimerical, but very real.

Whilst the word *Sorcery* has always seemed to me to be singularly elastic, it suggests to my mind an impression identical with that conveyed by *Magic*, with which I take it, in general, to be synonymous. Therefore, by sorcery I understand, and intend to convey, all those doctrines concerning the nature and power of angels and spirits ; the methods of evoking shades of departed persons ; the conjuration of elementary spirits and of demons ; the production of any kind of supernormal phenomena ; the making of talismans, potions, wands, etc. ; divination and crystallomancy ; and Cabalistic and ceremonial rites.

It may, perhaps, be said that no people has cultivated sorcery more assiduously than did the Chaldeans. The elaborate formulæ relating to demonology and possession which have been deciphered from the cuneiform, testify to the flourishing state of wizardry in Chaldea. But the elaborate and in many cases beautiful magic rituals formulated by the Egyptians for some reason possess a greater fascination for the modern student. Their system, indubitably, was more complete than any before or since.

Within the limits of this work it would be impossible even cursorily to scan the subject of sorcery in all its developments and in the guises lent to it by various nations. Therefore, I shall confine myself as closely as possible to those phases which we should bear in mind when we stand upon Calypso's island with Apollonius of Tyana and witness his translation from Rome ; when we disturb the ghostly studies of Nostradamus, seated upon his prophetic tripod ; when we intrude upon Count Cagliostro's Lodge of Isis, and, perceiving the beautiful Countess and thirty-six neophytes *in puris naturalibus*, retire in modest confusion.

I propose, now, to compare certain passages in *The Tales of the Magicians* (from Flinders Petrie's *Egyptian Tales*) with others in *The Thousand and One Nights*, in order to show that the traditions to this day regnant in the East have a genealogy which more often than not first started from the soil of Egypt.

In "Anpu and Bata" (*Egyptian Tales*) Bata is represented as placing his heart on the topmost flower of an acacia tree. By his heart is meant his *hati*—that is, more properly, his soul. This he did so that he could not be killed unless the tree were cut down. When the latter calamity occurred, the *hati* was found in a seed, which, being placed in a cup of water, expanded, and, his body reviving, he drank the water. He then changed into a sacred bull, which was sacrificed ; but two drops of its blood fell upon the ground, and these contained the *hati* or soul of Bata. They grew into two trees, which were cut down, but the *hati* passed into a shaving from one of them.

I shall invite you, next, to watch with me an encounter between rival sorcerers (actually, a sorceress and an *'efreet*) from *The Thousand and One Nights*, noting the curious analogies between the forms, animal and vegetable, into which the *hati*, or soul, retreats during the conflict. The episode will be found in "The Story of the Second Royal Mendicant."

SORCERY AND SORCERERS

The daughter of a certain King, who was acquainted with the secret arts, challenged " the 'Efreet Jarjarees, a descendant of Iblees," to mortal encounter, and, " taking a knife upon which were engraved some Hebrew names, marked with it a circle in the midst of the palace. Within this she wrote several names and talismans, and then she pronounced invocations, and uttered unintelligible words; and soon the palace around us " (I quote the Royal Mendicant) " became immersed in gloom to such a degree that we thought the whole world was overspread; and lo, the 'Efreet appeared before us in almost hideous shape, with hands like winnowing-forks, and legs like masts, and eyes like burning torches; so that we were terrified at him. The King's daughter exclaimed : ' No welcome to thee ! '—at which the 'Efreet, assuming the form of a lion . . . rushed upon the lady; but she instantly plucked a hair from her head and muttered with her lips, whereupon the hair became converted into a piercing sword, with which she struck the lion and he was cleft in twain by the blow; but his head became changed into a scorpion. The lady immediately transformed herself into an enormous serpent, and crept after the execrable wretch in the shape of a scorpion, and a sharp contest ensued between them, after which the scorpion became an eagle, and the serpent, changing to a vulture, pursued the eagle for a length of time. The latter then transformed himself into a black cat, and the King's daughter became a wolf, and they fought together long and fiercely, till the cat, seeing himself overcome, changed himself into a large, red pomegranate, which fell into a pool; but, the wolf pursuing it, it ascended into the air, and then fell upon the pavement of the palace, and broke in pieces, its grains becoming scattered, each apart from the others, and all spread about the whole space of ground enclosed by the palace. The wolf, upon this, transformed itself into a cock, in order to pick up the grains, and not leave one of them; but, according to the decree of fate, one grain remained hidden by the side of the pool of the fountain. The cock began to cry, and flapped its wings, and made a sign to us with its beak; but we understood not what it would say. It then uttered at us such a cry that we thought the whole palace had fallen down upon us;

and it ran about the whole of the ground, until it saw the grain that had lain hid by the side of the pool, when it pounced upon it to pick it up ; but it fell into the midst of the water, and became transformed into a fish, and sank into the water ; upon which the cock became a fish of a larger size and plunged in after the other. . . ."

II. THE BIRTH OF SORCERY

The persistent tradition that the secret lore of the Egyptian priests was written in certain " books " finds some slight confirmation in " Ahura's Tale," from the second series of *Egyptian Tales* ; for therein the *Book of Thoth* is thus described :

" He wrote it with his own hands and it will bring (raise) a man to the gods. To read two pages enables you to enchant the heaven, the earth, the abyss, the mountains and the sea ; you shall know what the birds of the sky and the crawling things are saying ; . . . And when the second page is read, if you are in the world of ghosts, you will grow again in the shape you were on earth. . . ."

The Brahmins, visited by Apollonius of Tyana, would seem to have possessed such a book, and the great sage himself claimed powers almost identical with those conferred by the *Book of Thoth*. But, concerning the latter, we read :

" This book is in the middle of the river at Koptos, in an iron box ; in the iron box is a bronze box ; in the bronze box is a sycamore box ; in the sycamore box is an ivory and ebony box ; in the ivory and ebony box is a silver box ; in the silver box is a golden box, and in that is the book. It is twisted all round with snakes and scorpions and all the other crawling things . . . and there is a deathless snake by the box."

The *Harris Papyrus* has references to similar magical books (nor must we overlook *The Book of Dzyan*, which Madame Blavatsky claimed to possess), but none of these ancient manuscripts affords us much help in tracing the origin of sorcery. That the Egyptian priesthood conserved the art through many generations, that we are indebted to them for their preservation of the traditions, is almost indisputable. But whence was their knowledge derived ? Research along ordinary lines has failed to enlighten us upon this point.

I shall venture, then, to cite here the views of a very advanced theosophical writer, but shall ask to be excused from any comment upon them :

We have to measure time by hundreds of thousands of years, he avers, if we endeavour to look back in imagination to the halcyon period of Egyptian civilization, and, by the use of figures on that scale, we are enabled to form an approximately correct conception of the origin of that wonderful structure, the Great Pyramid of Ghizeh, usually ascribed to a Pharaoh of the fourth dynasty, Cheops, or Khufu. Whilst he considers that many of the pyramids which decorate the banks of the Nile were really what Egyptologists suppose them to be—the tombs of kings, he believes that their form was adopted in imitation of that already exemplified by the early monument, dating back, even for the Egyptians of ten thousand years ago, to time immemorial.

The Great Pyramid, in this writer's opinion, is probably by far the oldest structure on earth. Its main purpose was to serve as a temple of initiation for those who were admitted to fellowship with the Atlantean Adepts, established in Egypt more than a hundred thousand years ago ! Its shape was designed to render it invulnerable to the geographical revolutions which were impending, and, in his own words, he " is given to understand " that since its erection it has actually been submerged beneath a northern inflow of the sea ; a consequence of an actual depression of the land now constituting Lower Egypt. But later undulations of the earth's crust in that region brought it to the surface again, uninjured and available in later times for the purposes to which it was originally assigned.

Great as the importance attaching to (really) Ancient Egypt undoubtedly may be, he continues, we must not imagine that the centre of occultism established there was by any means the only region from which the Adepts directed their watchfulness over mankind. When we talk about the catastrophes that shattered, and to a large extent destroyed, the ancient Atlantean continent, we are apt to forget that a good deal of existing land in the western hemisphere has survived those mighty changes.

A great deal of Mexico and Peru has transmitted to our own time architectural remains that he contends to be distinctly bequests of Atlantean civilization : and there is a region in Central America which, from the maturity of that civilization till now, has been and still is a centre from which Adept influence radiates over the world.[1]

III. THE HOME OF THE *GINN*

I have said that sorcery has come to us as a legacy from Ancient Egypt, and one of the most persistent traditions, instances of which appear from time to time in the press, has a foundation in the beautiful ritual known as *The Book of the Dead*. I refer to the uncanny properties ascribed to certain relics from the Nile land.

In the second series of Flinders Petrie's *Egyptian Tales* is a translation of a papyrus in the Ghizeh Museum, wherein we read :

" Now in the tomb was Na-Nefer-Ka-Ptah and with him was the *Ka* of his wife Ahura, for though she was buried at Koptos, her *Ka* dwelt at Memphis with her husband whom she loved."

The *Ka* is the Ego, and according to the Ancient Egyptian belief it could, at the death of the body, enter into any image or magical implement prepared for its reception. In the case cited above it dwelt in a statue, and the compiler of Volume VIII of the *Collectanea Hermetica* says :

" It seems exceedingly probable that as the mummy was the material basis for the *Sahu* (Astral form) and *Khaibt* (radiation), so the mummy-case with its painted presentment of the living person was the material basis for the preservation of the *Ka* of a low-grade initiate or the *Khu* (the magical powers) of a fully-equipped Adept."

Baron Textor de Ravisi says that " before the entire

---

[1] I understand that Yucatan is meant.

resurrection of the body the justified *Ka* could, if it chose, reanimate the body of the dead." This is almost identical with vampirism, where the corpse is found fresh in the tomb. The same authority has defined manifestations which are visible but intangible, whereof the head is distinctly visible but the limbs vaporous, to be composed of the Ego and the Soul. Those manifestations which resemble the bodily form of the deceased, but are intangible, are composed of the Ego and the Astral body; they are usually terrifying. Manifestations of the Will and the Instinct, re-united in the Spiritual body, are only visible to the spiritual sense; whilst manifestations procured through a medium are due to the *radiations* of the Astral body only, and possess none of the Ego, or individuality, of the deceased.

Certainly, the Egyptians had a more closely defined and altogether more comprehensible system than any since evolved; in fact, it is indubitable that many later systems are based upon it, being no more than worthless elaborations of the original.

Egypt was the wonderland of the ancient world, and by the all but unanimous testimony of the country's present inhabitants, the Nile land is still the theatre of singular supernatural happenings.

"In common with other countries of Islam," says Dr. Klunzinger (and this the *Koran* tells us), "Egypt is inhabited by a vast number of *ginn*. Like men they are born, mature, age and die. They are male and female, black or white, some high of station, some lowly; some are free and some slaves; Moslem and Christian." In short, they are parallel with mankind, from whom they are distinguished by their lack of flesh and blood, and by reason of their attaining to a great age—namely, three hundred years, or more.

Each child has a companion *ginn*, born in the same hour. This "familiar," or *Karina*, is female in the case of a male child, and male in the case of a female. A child who dies in infancy is said to have been killed by the *Karina*; and even in the official registers of deaths, until comparatively recently, the *Karina* was frequently entered as a recognized ailment.

Usually the *ginn* are said to be invisible; but they

can assume all kinds of intangible and vapoury forms, with the resemblances of men, animals, and monsters. When a proper view is obtained of them they may at once be distinguished by their perpendicular eye.

The art of calling up these dread beings, in order to exorcise them, or to make them do one's bidding by invoking them by name, is cultivated throughout the Moslem world by great numbers of men, and by some women. By the instrumentality of the *ginn*, the "servants of the secret," or by the knowledge of one of the "secret names of God," those acquainted with occult lore can perform miracles. That the greater number of these Moslem sorcerers are poor men—often mendicants— may, therefore, appear remarkable ; but it is claimed that self-denial is essential in a compact with a *ginn*. Some sorcerers of Moslem Egypt are said to be formally married to a *ginnee*, or female *ginn*, and to perform their wonders by means of their supernatural spouse.

A mysterious Moslem gentleman suspected of being wedded to a *ginnee* appeared in Egypt in the early part of the nineteenth century, styling himself Säid Abd-el-Rahmán el Adàros, and claiming to have come from India. He sailed up the Nile with a vessel and extensive retinue, and proclaimed that he designed to travel in the Sudan. Eye-witnesses swore to having seen him take pieces of money from beneath his carpet whenever he so willed, and that he could with a breath change silver coins into gold ones. Suffice it that the mysterious gentleman was denounced to the Government as a sorcerer and escorted from the country !

An old Moslem authority says: "Let a Christian beware of calling up a Moslem *ginn*. The *ginn* will avenge himself for this affront and immediately put his summoner to death."

In the modern magic books of the East we read how to gain the affections of another ; to awake at will ; to unfasten chains ; to recapture an escaped slave ; to keep a wife from faithlessness ; to cause the belly of a thief to swell up ; to make a man or an ox pursue him ; to discover buried treasure ; to call up *ginn* ; to find pieces of gold under one's pillow. I will instance a charm for calling up *ginn*: the *naïveté* of the concluding sentence is quaint.

Fast for seven days, and let body and clothes be clean. Read first the chapter of the *Koran*, " the Angel," to the word *hazîr*, fourteen times after the sunset prayer; then pray with four genuflections, uttering the *fatha* seven times at each, and when on the seventh night you have read that chapter fourteen times, ask of God whatsoever you wish. The *ginn*, who are the servants of this chapter, will now appear " and will give you information *respecting the treasure and how you may obtain possession of it.*"

A certain individual, who asserted that he had undergone such a course of self-mortification and spirit-seeking, informed the author of *Upper Egypt* that he had seen all kinds of horrible forms in his magic circle, but that he saw them also when his eyes were shut. At last, becoming quite terrified, he fled from the place.

The following is said to be a love-charm :

" On a Wednesday after the Vesper prayer, and when your shadow measures twenty paces, write the following formula (*châtim*) with rose-water and sesame water on paper or parchment. Roll this up and throw it on the ground. Then write the formula on the palm of the left hand and fumigate with mastic, benzoin, and coriander. Say over the chapters *Amran* and *Ichlâs* while your hand is held above the smoke, and then pick up the talisman from the ground. Touch your body with it, and that of the person on whom you have designs. Hang it to . . . your right side, and you will see something wonderful. God's protection is with thee. But use the talisman only for what is lawful ! "

The magic mirror enjoys great popularity. A boy (not more than twelve years of age), a virgin, or a black female slave is directed to look into a cup filled with water or into a pool of ink ; the *skryer* is furthermore fumigated with incense, whilst certain sentences are murmured by the magician. After a time, when the boy (for a boy is usually employed) is asked what he sees, he reports that he sees persons moving in the mirror. The magician orders the boy to lay certain commands on the spirit. The commands are obeyed at once. The magician asks the spectators to name any person whom they would wish to appear in the mirror, no matter whether the person be living or dead. The boy commands the spirit to bring the individual desired. In a few seconds he is present, and the boy proceeds to describe him.

"Which description, however, according to our own observation," says one writer, "is always quite wide of the mark." But E. W. Lane's experiments in this art (called *darb-el-mendel*) with the Sheikh Abd-El-Kadir El-Maghrabee, as recounted in *The Modern Egyptians*, may be consulted as a check to this opinion.

An account of a curious case of magic in Cairo, during the last century, may be given here, to show how great a degree of faith the Egyptians in general place in the arts of enchantment.

Moustafa Ed-Digwee, chief secretary in the Cadi's Court, in Cairo, was dismissed from his office, and succeeded by another person of the name of Moustafa, who had been a money-changer. The former sent a petition to the Pasha, begging to be reinstated ; but before he received an answer he was attacked by a severe illness, which he believed to be the effect of enchantment : he persuaded himself that Moustafa the money-changer had employed a magician to write a spell which should cause him to die ; and therefore sent a second time to the Pasha charging the new secretary with this crime.

The accused was brought before the Pasha, and confessed that he had had resort to malign arts, naming the magician whom he had employed. The latter was arrested, and, being unable to deny the charge brought against him, was thrown into prison, where he was sentenced to remain until it should be seen whether or not Ed-Digwee would die.

He was confined in a small cell, at the door of which two soldiers were placed in turn to watch over the prisoner. Lane, in dealing with this incident, says :

"Now for the marvellous part of the story.

"At night, after one of the guards had fallen asleep, the other heard a strange, murmuring noise, and, looking through a crack of the door of the cell, saw the magician sitting in the middle of the floor, muttering some words which he (the guard) could not understand. Presently

B

the candle which was before him became extinguished ; and, at the same instant, four other candles appeared, one in each corner of the cell.

" The magician then rose, and, standing on one side of the cell, knocked his head three times against the wall ; and each time that he did so, the wall opened and a man appeared to come forth from it. After the magician had conversed for some minutes with the three personages whom he had thus produced, they disappeared ; as did, also, the four candles ; and the candle that was in the midst of the cell became lighted again, as at first : the magician then resumed his position on the floor, and all was quiet. Thus the spell that was to have killed Ed-Digwee was dissolved.

" Early next morning, the invalid felt himself so much better that he called for a basin and ewer, performed the ablution, and said his prayers ; and from that time he rapidly recovered. He was restored to his former office ; and the magician was banished from Egypt."

IV. THE SIBYLS

We shall see, presently, that not only Apollonius of Tyana, but also Dee, Nostradamus, and Cagliostro were notable, chiefly, as prophets. If divination be but elementary magic, it is more highly esteemed by the layman than by the student, and the Sibylline lights flare dimly through the darkness of to-day, as flared such smoky torches in the blacker gloom of Babylon, Memphis, Delphi, Rome.

Therefore, whoever would seek for pearls in the ocean of obscurity which overtides the history of oracular manifestation must arm against the influences of modern environment and modern thought ; must recede from this age of sceptics, through the middle ages of fanatic Christianity, pass by the birth of the New Creed, by the death of the gods, and take pause before the Capitol of Rome at what time Cæsar makes his last visit to the Senate House.

THE SIBYLS

It must be remembered that Rome, during the centuries of her ascendancy, gave to the world some of the keenest intellects, some of the most highly-trained observers whose laurelled images adorn man's gallery of genius. If we discredit the opinions of such as these because of the pagan credulity of the age they ornamented, we err ; for were they not more advantageously circumstanced to weigh in the balance the omen of the soothsayer, whose eyes attested to the justice of his warning ; to accept or reject the pronouncements of the Sibyls, who themselves had converse with these mystic sisters ; who, as Æneas at Cumæ, heard the words spoken by Herophile from the cavern ; who—some among them—lived to see the Oracle fulfilled ?

Since in the wheel of the centuries Rome is the hub, and, in any retrospective criticism, scarce may we see beyond its shadow, our inquiry concerning the ancient Oracles fairly may be said to centre upon the seven hills. The Sibyls claim priority, of course ; and therefore at this point a brief survey of the Sibylline traditions prevalent in Ancient Rome may not be out of place.

First, the Persian ; the Libyan ; the Delphian ; the Cimmerian in Italy ; the Erythræan, said to have foretold the fall of Troy ; the Samian ; the far-famed Cumæan, who brought the famous " nine books " to King Tarquinius Priscus ; the Hellespontine ; the Phrygian ; the tenth was the Tiburtine, named Albunea, worshipped at Tibur (modern Tivoli). To Lactantius we are indebted for this item of information : " Of all these Sibyls, the songs are both made public and held in use except those of the Cumæan, whose books are kept secret by the Romans ; neither do they hold it lawful for them to be inspected by any but the fifteen men." These fifteen men were, of course, the Quindecemviri, or college of priests, to whom the care of the Sibylline books were entrusted at Rome.

From the fact of the concealment of the Cumæan Oracles it has been contended, contrary from the opinion of Pliny, who says that the Sibylline books were destroyed by fire in the year 83 B.C., that none were lost in the burning of the Capitol but the Cumæan, since none but the Cumæan were concealed there. But, in addition to these, there were kept in the Capitol some Oracles prescribed by the Pythia at Delphi ; so that some doubt must always prevail respecting the fate of the Delphic as well as of the Cumæan Oracles.

As to the time when the several Sibyls lived, again we find contrary opinions, conflicting evidences, and irreconcilable accounts. If Osopæus be worthy of credence, then, according to him, the Sibyl at Delphi was a Phrygian, " more ancient than Orpheus." One Sibyl lived in the time of the Jewish Judges ; the Cumæan, in the time of Amasias ; the Samian, in the time of Josiah. There was a Sibyl in Samos in the time of Darian Astyages, and the Sibylla Cumana prophesied in the Fiftieth Olympiad, or the Fifty-fourth. " The Delphica is the oldest Sibyl," we read, " and lived before the Trojan War. Homer borrowed many of her verses." But against this we have the opinion of Gallæus, who thought that the Sibyls plagiarized Homer !

The one substantial datum which may be established is this : the Sibyls, whether justly or as a result of a species of auto-hypnosis, believed themselves to be inspired and were believed to be inspired by generations of Greek and Roman philosophers and thinkers. So much for their pretensions.

As to their later acceptance by contemporary authorities, a moment's consideration of the facts available—and these are multitudinous—will reveal how they were accepted without question until that same state of affairs became regnant in Rome which rules among ourselves to-day.

The false Oracles of the temple of Isis, unveiled, intact in all their trickery, by the spade of the excavator at Pompeii, afford but one instance among many. The Romans saw impostors practising false oracular mummery about them ; and as to-day none but the superstitious are disposed to hearken to the Sibyls of Bond Street, so, in that distant yesterday, it came about that none but the gullible and the morbid remained susceptible to the pseudo-wisdom of such false prophets as those of Pompeii. The true was mutilated by the false until the true was lost. Once lost it was all but forgotten, and at last its very existence was denied.

THE SIBYLS

The wonders attributed to the Sibyl who lived in the cave at Cumæ are an instance of how the possibly true may be so overlaid by the false and apocryphal that, to one looking back in quest of verity, the true has become but dimly perceptible, if perceptible at all.

Of this Cumæan Sibyl it was related that Apollo had become enamoured of her, and had offered to grant her whatever she might ask of him. She asked that she should be permitted to live for as many years as she held grains of sand in her hand. The god at once granted her request, but then she refused to reciprocate his love. Therefore he pronounced that her long life should be to her a curse rather than a blessing, for that she should be without freshness and beauty. She was reputed to be seven hundred years old when Æneas came to Italy, but doomed to live nearly as many more ere the number of her years would equal the sands she had held ; and her ultimate destiny was to wither away and become only a voice.

However, the Delphic Oracle is preserved to us in Herodotus (vi. 86). Glaucus, son of Epicydes, is said to have received from the Milesians a large sum of money, and to have given a pledge to restore it when properly demanded. When, however, the demand was made, Glaucus professed to be ignorant of any such obligation. Whilst the matter was pending, he went to Delphi and consulted the Pythian Oracle, receiving the following response :

> Glaucus of Epicydes, greater gain
> Immediate is it by oath to overcome,
> And take the money as by force ; swear then,
> Since death awaits the man that keeps his oath.
> But Orcus has a nameless son, nor hands
> Nor feet are his, bur swift he moves along,
> Till, having seized a whole race, he destroys,
> And all the house. But the race of man
> Who keeps his oath is better afterward.

In common with the great majority of such Oracles, this response is characterized by a predominant element of uncertainty and enigmatical obscurity, leavened with a pinch of sound advice.

Not even the new thought that exercised a revolutionary intellectual influence in the dawn of Christianity could quench the light of the Oracles. Few among the early Christian writers would seem to have doubted the authenticity of the Sibyls ; and no further reference is necessary here to the power which these mystic books exercised over the whole of pagan Greece and Rome.

V. ORIENTAL ORACLES

Although, in Roman times, the Egyptian Oracles became so debased, it should not be forgotten that during the height of Egypt's grandeur the policy of the kingdom was largely, if not wholly, dictated by the pronouncements of the mouthpiece of the gods, or first prophet. Egyptian history contains the names of numberless such prophets. The prophets were the high priests, and though the Pharaoh ruled Egypt the high priest ruled Pharaoh. Whether or not the prophecies of the priests of Amen were inspired, they, *sans doute,* were dictated by a shrewd regard for the welfare of the community and informed with a forceful statesmanship that must command the student's admiration.

In the reign of Shepses-Ka-f, we read of one Ptah-Shepses, who was the " prophet of the god Sekar " and (from which his influence may be adjudged) " chief of the priesthood of Memphis." The Sphinx, too, was regarded as prophetic, and an inscription upon it tells us that " . . . a great enchantment rests upon this place from the beginning of time, as far as the districts of the lords of Babylon, the sacred road of the gods to the western horizon of On-Heliopolis, because the form of the Sphinx is a likeness of Sheper-ra, the very great god who abides at this place, the greatest of all spirits, the most venerable being who rests upon it."

Tehuti-mes IV ascribed his elevation to the throne to the active protection and aid of the oracular Horem-Khu ; and the inscription upon the memorial stone before the breast of the Sphinx tells us how, " when hunting lions in the valley of the gazelles," he rested in the shadow of this potent one's image. "It seemed to him as though this great god spoke to him with his own mouth."

Here, it is difficult to decide whether the Sphinx should be regarded as oracular, whether the true Oracle was Tehuti-mes, or whether the alleged communication of the god was no more than a cloak to hide the prince's intrigue to secure the throne. Be this as it may, he caused it to be proclaimed that the god had said to him, ". . . Thou shalt wear the white crown and the red crown. . . . The world shall be thine in its length and in its breadth . . . the sand of the district in which I have my existence has covered me up. Promise me that thou wilt do what I wish. . . ." When Tehuti-mes IV came to the throne, certainly he kept the promise which he had made, thought he had made, or averred that he had made, to the oracular deity; he cleared away the accumulated sand and freed from its confinement the gigantic body of the Sphinx.

Throughout the eastern nations, this yearning to know the unknowable—which, indeed, is inherent in modern western man to this day—exhibited itself constantly. It was this trait of Oriental character that made the institution of prophets, seers, and Oracles an essential part of the scheme of things. In Assyrian history, it is related that Esarhaddon, being hard pressed by a group of nations to the north-east of Assyria, led by a certain Kashtariti, and among whose followers the Gimirites, the Medes and Manneans were the most prominent, asked for an Oracle from Shamash regarding the outcome of the situation. The priest, acting as mediator, thus addressed the god :

"O Shamash! great Lord! As I ask thee do thou in mercy answer me. From this day, the third day of this month of Iyan, to the eleventh day of the month of Ab of this year, a period of one hundred days and one hundred nights, is the prescribed term for the priestly activity. Will within this period Kashtariti, together with his soldiery, will the army of the Gimirites, the army of the Medes, will the army of the Manneans, or will any enemy whatsoever succeed in carrying out their plan, whether by strategy or by main force, whether by the force of weapons of war and fight or by the axe, whether by breach made with machines of war and battering rams or by hunger, whether by the power residing in the name of a god or goddess, whether in a friendly way, or by friendly grace, or by any strategic device, will these aforementioned, as many as are required to take a city, actually capture the city of Kishsassu, penetrate into the interior of that same city of Kishsassu, so that it falls into their power? Thy great divine power knows it. The capture of that same city of Kishsassu, through any enemy whatsoever, within the specified period, is it definitely ordained by thy great and divine will, O Shamash ?   Will it actually come to pass ? "

The exact phraseology and exhaustive character of this invocation would reflect little discredit upon an up-to-date solicitor !

Pausanius tells us that the Oracle of Hermes at Pharæ was " the casual utterances of men."   One who wished to consult the Oracle came in the evening to the statue of Hermes in the market-place, that stood beside a hearth altar to which bronze lamps were attached. Having kindled the lamps and put a piece of money on the altar, he whispered into the ear of the statue whatsoever he desired to know, and departed, closing his ears with his hands. Whatever human speech he first heard on removing them, he accepted as an Oracle.

The famed Pythoness of Delphi appears to have chewed leaves of the sacred laurel and then to have drunk water from the prophetic stream called Kassotis, which flowed underground. But the height of the afflatus was attained when she seated herself upon the tripod ; and here she was supposed to be inspired by a mystic vapour that arose from a fissure in the ground.

Shortly after the defeat of Mohammed by the Coreish (the Meccans) at Ohod, a scene occurred which illumines the manner in which the Oracles of Mohammed were given to the Faithful.

Among the slain was Sàd, son of Rabi, a leader of the Bani Khazraj. He left a widow and two daughters ; but his brother, in accordance with the practice of the times, took possession of the entire inheritance. The widow—not unnaturally—was grieved at this ; and, being a discreet and prudent woman, determined to obtain redress, if redress were obtainable. Accordingly she invited the Prophet to a feast, with some twenty of his intimates. A retired spot among the palm trees of the widow's garden was well sprinkled with water, and the repast spread.

Mohammed arrived, and with his companions took his seat upon the carpets prepared. Sympathetically he spoke to the widow of her bereavement, with such pathos that all the women wept, and the eyes of the Prophet himself filled with tears. The supper disposed of, a feast of fresh dates followed ; whereupon the widow arose, and addressed her guest as follows :

" Sàd, as thou well knowest, was slain at Ohod. His brother hath seized the inheritance. There is nothing left for the two daughters ; and how shall they be married without a portion ? "

Mohammed, much moved by the simple tale, replied :

" The Lord shall decide regarding the inheritance ; for no command hath yet been revealed to me in this matter. Come again unto me when I shall have returned home." With this he departed.

Later, as with his companions he rested at the door of his own house, symptoms of inspiration came upon him— he was oppressed, and we are told that the drops of sweat fell like pearls from his forehead. Then he commanded that the widow of Sàd and his brother should be summoned ; and when they were brought before him, he pronounced thus :

" Restore unto the daughter of Sàd two-thirds of that which he hath left behind him and one-eighth part for his widow ; the remainder is for thee."

The widow, rejoicing, then uttered the Takbir, " Great is the Lord ! "

VI. EXTRAORDINARY MODES OF DIVINATION

I have dealt at some length with what I may term " official " Oracles for the reason that the subject bears so directly upon the life of Nostradamus, as will presently appear ; for Michel de Notre Dame became, in a sense, the official prophet of France. Before we dismiss altogether the subject of divination, we might profitably glance at some of the more extraordinary windows of futurity opened by peering mankind ; for the doings of the seer have enriched the annals of occultism with some singular pages. Thus, Julian the Apostate, in his necromantic practices and nocturnal sacrifices, is said to have immolated many children in order to consult their intestines (*anthropomancy*).

When he was at Carra, in Mesopotamia, he is said to have retired to the Temple of the Moon with some companions, and, his mystic operations concluded, to have left the temple locked and sealed, and with a guard over the door. He never returned to Carra, being slain in the war ; and when, in the reign of Jovian, the place was opened, a woman was found hanging by her hair, her hands outstretched, her body cut open and the liver removed.

Divination by means of table-turning was known to the Egyptian priests, apparently from the earliest times. It has come to us by way of Rome, for to the Romans the practice passed.

The instrument known as *planchette* is no more than a variation of the gyrating table ; and tripod-turning enjoyed a considerable vogue in Rome, when the Romans I presume, had tired of the original Egyptian form of the practice (the gyrating of a kind of sieve).

Tertullian speaks of those who, " putting their faith in angels or demons, made goats and even tripods prophesy to them."

This table-turning of Old Rome, however, was invested with all the pomp of religious ceremonial ; being indeed a wholly demoniacal business. In the report of the confession of certain conspirators who, under Valens, had consulted a prophetic tripod (*dactylomancy*) as a preliminary measure to that of assassinating the Emperor, we find the conspirators saying :

" We have constructed this accursed little tripod, most sublime judges, in the semblance of the Delphic tripod, and we have fashioned it, with solemn incantations, from the branches of a consecrated laurel. In accordance with ancient custom, we have surrounded it with divers ornaments, and consecrated it by means of imprecations charms, and mystic verses; and this being done, we *moved* it."

The report further tells us how the conspirators purified the apartment in which the mystic rites were to be performed. Around the edge of the metal basin in which the tripod was to be turned, were engraved, at equal distances one from another, the twenty-four letters of the alphabet.

In the form of the ensuing ceremony, and in the part played by these twenty-four letters, we perceive a certain similarity between this tripod and the *planchette*. For the officiating priest (robed in white linen and with shaven skull, and bearing a sprig of vervain in his hand) took note of the letters which were struck by the rings suspended from the table, as it turned about.

Upon this occasion the rings struck *Th* and *E* in reply to the conspirators' query as to who was to succeed Valens. This was taken as a confirmation of the popular belief that Theodorus should be the future Emperor. I now come to the really notable part of this episode in the history of sorcery.

Valens, at this time, found himself equally curious for reliable information upon this matter of the succession, and had recourse to the magical art of *alectromancy*.

A cock (he should have been white and deprived of his claws) was placed within a circle marked about with the letters of the alphabet, covered with grain, from which the bird was allowed to peck at discretlon. In this way, the cock laid bare the letters *Th, E, O,* and *D*. The Emperor seems to have entertained no doubt that *Theodorus* was the name indicated, since he promptly had Theodorus put to death. The existence of *Theodosius* had been overlooked, alike by the conspirators and by Valens, and Theodosius succeeded to the Empire.

Animal magnetism, in one form or another, plays an important part in many sorceries. In Cochin-China there exist those who, it is said, are able, solely by the effort of their will, to propel heavy barges! I will not cite the authority responsible for this statement, but pass on to the account of an eye-witness of some of the phenomena at command of the Lamas of Tibet; for the arts of Tibet are indissolubly bound up with the fame of Madame Blavatsky.

One of the feats related is as follows:

In order to discover a criminal, the Lama seats himself upon the ground before a small, square table, on which he lays his hand, whilst he chants from a certain book. After a time he rises, lifting his hand; whereupon the table is likewise seen to rise, following his hand—until it has risen to the level of the Lama's eyes.

It next commences a rotary motion; and its speed becomes so great that he appears hard put to it to follow, even by running. Finally, having pursued various directions, the table falls. Its fall is said to indicate the point of the compass toward which search should be made for the culprit.

The traveller whose account has furnished me with the foregoing, avers that he was four times a witness of this surprising feat. Search failed, however, to bring the culprit (in this case a thief) to light; until, when the quest had been abandoned, a man resident in the indicated direction killed himself. The stolen property, we are told, was discovered to be concealed in his hut!

In conclusion I may mention an account of *Bokte* sorcery for which we are indebted to the French traveller, M. Huc. According to the latter, a *Bokte* of the Lama convent of Rache-Churin, to a wild vocal accompaniment by brother Lamas, ripped himself entirely open with a sacred scimitar, and, during his sufferings, submitted to interrogation anent the future —his answers being regarded as oracular.

The devout curiosity of the pilgrims (who flock to these bloody ceremonies) being satisfied, M. Huc tells us that the *Bokte* passes his hand rapidly over his stomach, and it " becomes as whole as it was before," without the slightest trace remaining of the diabolical operation—with the exception of an extreme lassitude ! [1]

VII. " THE ENIGMA OF THE SPHINX "

Sorcery, or that form of sorcery which may be termed ceremonial, owes its survival, in a great measure, to Alphonse Louis Constant or " Éliphas Lévi." I consider that Éliphas Lévi may justly be called the last of the

[1] An Indian doctor with whom I am acquainted has himself witnessed an identical experiment.

sorcerers. Yet, outside the study of the student of occultism, Lévi is unknown. How many readers of *A Strange Story, Zanoni*, and *The Haunters and the Haunted*, are aware that the author was one of the privileged few whom the great master of magic accepted as disciples, was a pupil of Éliphas Lévi ? Lord Lytton as a sorcerer, is an unfamiliar figure ; nevertheless, as a sorcerer, and an Adept, he is regarded by those qualified to judge.

Possibly an explanation of Lévi's mystical and misleading phraseology is to be found in his *Magical Ritual* (translated from MSS. and edited by W. Wynn Westcott, M.B.). In the chapter, " The Tower—La Maison de Dieu," we read :

" Do you know why the Fiery Sword of Samael is stretched over the Garden of Delight, which was the cradle of our race ?

" Do you know why the Deluge was ordered to efface from the earth every vestige of the race of the giants ?

" Do you know why the Temple of Solomon was destroyed ?

" These events have been necessary because the Great Arcanum of the Knowledge of Good and of Evil has been revealed.

" Angels have fallen because they have attempted to divulge this Great Secret. It is the secret of Life, and when its first word is betrayed that word becomes fatal. If the Devil himself were to uttter that word, he would die."

This word, we are told, will destroy each one who speaks it and everyone who hears it spoken. If it were spoken aloud in the hearing of the people of a town, that town would be given over to anathema. If that word were to be whispered beneath the dome of a temple, then within three days the temple doors would fly open, a Voice would utter a cry, the divine occupant would depart, and the building would fall in ruins. No refuge could be found for one who revealed it ; if he mounted to the topmost part of a tower, the lightning flash would strike him ; if he tried to hide himself in the caverns of the earth, a torrent would whirl him away ; if he sought refuge in the house of a friend, he would be betrayed ; if in the arms of the wife of his bosom, she would desert him in affright.

In his passion of despair he would renounce his science and knowledge, and, condemning himself to the same blindness as did Œdipus, would shriek out—" I have profaned the bed of my mother ! "

" Happy is the man who solves the Enigma of the Sphinx, but wretched is he who retails the answer to another."

He who has solved the secret and guards its secrecy is described as the " King of Earth " ; he disdains mere riches, is inaccessible to any suffering or fear from destiny ; he could wait with a smile the crash of worlds. This secret is, moreover, profaned and falsified by its mere revelation, and never yet has a just or a true idea come from its betrayal. " Those who possess it have found it. Those who pronounce it for others to hear have lost it— already."

Those who would understand the mysteries and perform miracles are warned by Éliphas Lévi to weigh well their knowledge and power ere entering upon the attempt ; for if they be in any way deficient, he says, they stand upon the brink of an abyss.

" But if you have secured the Lamp and Wand of Initiation, if you are cognizant of the secrets of the Nine, if you never speak to God without the Light which proceeds from Him, if you have received the mystical baptism of the Four Elements, if you have prayed upon the Seven Mountains, if you know the mode of motion of the Double Sphinxed Chariot, if you have grasped the dogma of why Osiris was a black god, if you are free, if you are a King, if you are in truth a priest in the Temple of Solomon— act without fear, and speak, for your words will be all-powerful in the spiritual kingdom. . . ."

Furthermore, however, it is necessary to know the names and powers of the twelve precious jewels which are included in the crown of gold of the sun, and the names of the chief powers of the moon. Also, one must be familiar with the keys of the Fifty Gates, the secret of the Thirty-two Paths, and the characters of the Seven Spirits.

Incense plays a very important part in ritualistic sorcery, as it played an important part in Egyptian sorcery. Thus : for conjurations on Sunday the incense should be cinnamon, frankincense, saffron, and red sandal-wood. For Monday : camphor, white sandal-wood, amber, and cucumber seeds. For Thursday: ambergris, cardamom, " grains of paradise," balm, mace, and saffron ; and so on.

It may be of interest to mention here the constituents of *Kyphi*, the celebrated incense of Ancient Egypt. A recipe for its preparation is contained in the Ebers papyrus, and Ebers says that three different varieties were made up by L. Voigt, a Berlin chemist. That from the formula of Dioscorides was the best. It consisted of resin, wine, *Rad. Galangæ*,[1] juniper berries, root of aromatic rush, asphaltum, mastic, myrrh, Burgundy grapes, and honey.

Lévi says of the Seal of Solomon :

" It consists in the interlaced triangles ; the erect triangle is of flame colour, the inverse triangle is coloured blue. In the centre space there may be drawn a Tau cross and three Hebrew Yods, or a *crux ansata* (*ankh*), or the Triple Tau of the Arch-masons. He who with Intelligence and Will is armed with this emblem has need of no other thing ; he should be all-potent, for this is the perfect sign of the Absolute."

Éliphas Lévi also instructs us upon the formation and consecration of the Magic Wand. He who would possess it must select the wood of an almond or nut tree which has just flowered for the first time ; the bough should be cut off at one blow by the " magical sickle." It must be bored evenly from end to end without causing any crack or injury, and a magnetized steel needle of the same length as the bough must be introduced. One end must be closed by a clear, transparent glass bead, and the other end by a similar bead of resin : the ends should be covered then with sachets of silk. Two rings must next be fitted near the middle of the wand, one of copper and one of zinc, and two lengths of fine copper chain rolled around the wand. Upon the wand should then be written the names of the Twelve Spirits of the Zodiacal Cycle, with their sigils added :

Aries	Sarahiel
Taurus	Araziel
Gemini	Saraiel
Cancer	Phakiel
Leo	Seratiel
Virgo	Schaltiel

[1] Galangal root.

<pre>
Libra   .   .   .   Chadakiel
Scorpio .   .   .   Sartziel
Sagittarius   .   .   Saritiel
Capricornus   .   .   Semaqiel
Aquarius .   .   .   Tzakmaqiel
Pisces   .   .   .   Vacabiel
</pre>

Finally, upon the copper ring must be engraved in Hebrew letters, from right to left, the words " The Holy Jerusalem," H QDShH JRUShLIM ; and upon the zinc ring in Hebrew letters, from right to left, the words " The King Solomon," H MLK ShLMH, Heh Melek Shelomoh.

When the wand is complete, it must be consecrated by the invocations of the Spirits of the Four Elements and the Seven Planets, by ceremonies lasting over the seven days of a week, using the special incense and prayers for each day.

The consecrated wand, in common with all magical instruments, should be kept wrapped in silk, and never allowed in contact with any colour but black. The ideal receptacle for it is a cedar or ebony box.

With this wand, duly made and fully consecrated, " the Magus can cure unknown diseases, he may enchant a person or cause him to fall asleep at will, can wield the forces of the elements and cause the Oracles to speak."

VIII.   THE SOUL OF THE WORLD

I shall now draw your attention to the philosophy of the last of the Magi, as expounded in that chapter of *The Magical Ritual* called " L'Amoureux " :

He enjoins us to bear in mind that equilibrium results only from the opposition of forces, the active having no existence without the passive ; that light without darkness is formless ; and " Yea " can win no triumph save over " Nay." Love, also, gains added strength from hate, and hell is the hotbed of such plants as shall bear root in heaven.

He tells us, too, that the great Fluidic Agent which is called the " Soul of the World," and which is represented with the horned head of the Cow of Isis to express animal fecundity, is a *blind* force.

The power which the Magus wields is composed of two opposing forces, which unite in love and disjoin in discord ; love associating contraries, whilst hate makes of similars rivals and enemies. Hatred succeeds to love when by saturation the void has become filled, "unless the full cannot become empty"; but the usual result is an " equilibrated saturation, due to mutual repulsions."

Sexual love the Magus regards as a physical manifestation ; repugnance and pain may be forgotten by those who are under its sway. This is a form of inebriation arising from the attraction of two contrary fluids ; and at the conjunction of the positive and negative poles there results an ecstasy and orgasm during which the loved one seems the brilliant phantom of a vision.

Our consideration is solicited for the bodily and mental disorders which result from solitude and its accompanying fluidic congestions, due to want of equilibrium : such as nervous maladies, hysteria, hypochondriasis, megrim, vapours, and insane delusions. It becomes possible, in the light of the new wisdom, to understand the ailments of maidens, and of women of an uncertain age, of widows and of celibates.

Inspired by this natural law of equilibrium, " you may often predict the future course of a life, and may cure many such ailments, often by distracting the attention when unduly fixed, and so may the Magus become as great a physician as Paracelsus, or as renowned a diviner as was Cornelius Agrippa. You will come to understand the diseases of the soul ; the fact that learned and chaste persons often hunger after the pleasures of vice will be noticed, and so will it be observed that men and women steeped in vices turn at times to the consolations of virtue ; and thus you may predict the occurrence of strange conversions and of unexpected sins, and great astonishment will be shown at your facility in discerning the most carefully concealed secrets of the heart and home.

" Girls and women may be by such means of divination shown in dreams the forms of lover and husband ; such confidantes are potent auxiliaries in magic arts ; never abuse their position, never neglect their interests, for they

C

are good gifts to the Magus. In order to possess an assured sway over the heads and hearts of women, it is essential to obtain the favour of both Gabriel, the Angel of the Moon, and of Anäel, the Angel of Venus."

Certain female evil demons must be overcome and cast down in order that perfect equilibrium be established. Foremost of these are :

Nahémah, princess of the Succubi.

Lilith, queen of the Stryges, tempting to debauchery, and destroyer of maternal desire.

" Nahémah presides also over illicit and sterile caresses.

" Lilith rejoices in strangling in their cradles children whose origin has been soiled by the touch of Nahémah."

The truly wise master of the Cabala, we are told, understands the concealed meaning of these names, and of such demoniac evil powers, which are also called the material envelopes or cortices or shells of the Tree of Life, soiled and blackened by the outer darkness ; they are as branches which are dead, having been torn off the tree, whence issue light, life, and love.

Finally, these, according to Lévi, are some of the privileges of a Magus :

Aleph.—He sees God and is able to commune with the seven Genii around the throne.

Vau.—He understands the reasons for the Present, the Past, and the Future.

Zain.—He holds the secret of what is meant by the resurrection from the dead.

A few of his powers are these :

Cheth.—The power of making the Philosopher's Stone.

Teth.—The possession of the Universal Medicine.

Samech.—To know in a moment the hidden thoughts of any man or woman.

Peh.—To foresee any future events which do not depend upon the will of a superior being.

Resh.—Never to feel love or hatred unless it is designed.

Shin.—To possess the secret of constant wealth, and never to fall into destitution or misery.

These privileges are the final degree of Human Perfectibility ; these are open to attainment by the elect, by those who can dare, by those who would never abuse them and who know when to be silent.

IX. THE ELEMENTALS

It will be seen that this form of sorcery has to do largely with the doctrine of Elemental Spirits. The existence of such intelligences has been credited from the earliest times, and the *ginn* and *'efreet* of Arabian lore are Elementals under another name.

There are early Assyrian incantations addressed to Elementals, and the 108th chapter of the Ancient Egyptian *Book of the Dead* is called " The Chapter of Knowing the Spirits of the West."

According to the Abbé de Villars, the air is full of an innumerable multitude of creatures of human form, somewhat fierce of aspect, but in reality tractable, great lovers of the sciences, excessively subtle, eager to serve the sage, but hostile to the fool. Their wives and daughters are beauties of a masculine type, and may be likened to the Amazons. The seas and rivers are thus inhabited as well as the air, and the beings who dwell therein were denominated Nymphs or Undines by the Adepts of the past. Few males are born to them, but the women are numerous, and they are very beautiful, so that the daughters of men cannot compare with them. The earth, too, is populated to a point within a short distance of its centre with Gnomes, who are people of a low stature, the guardians of buried treasure, of mines, and of gems. They are ingenious, amicable toward mankind, and may be commanded with ease. " They supply the Children of the Sages with the money which they need, and desire no other wages for their labours but the glory of the service."

The Gnomides, their wives, are diminutive, but exceptionally pretty, and very quaint in their attire. Regarding the Salamanders, or igneous inhabitants of the fiery region, they serve the philosophers, but do not court their company, and their wives and daughters are even more elusive. The wives of the Salamanders, however, are more beautiful than any of the other Elementals, for their element is purer, and " you will be even more charmed with the beauty of their minds than with their physical perfections.

" Yet you cannot but pity these helpless creatures when I tell you that their souls are mortal, and that they have no hopes of enjoying that Eternal Being whom they know and religiously adore. Composed of the purest parts of the elements which they inhabit, and having no opposing qualities, they subsist, it is true, for many ages ; yet what is time in comparison with eternity ? They must eventually return to the abyss of oblivion. So much does this knowledge afflict them that they are frequently inconsolable. But God, whose mercy is infinite, revealed to our fathers, the philosophers, a remedy for this evil. They learned that in the same manner that man, by the alliance which he hath contracted with God, hath been made a partaker in divinity, so may the Sylphs, Gnomes, Undines, and Salamanders, by an alliance with man, be made partakers of immortality and of the bliss to which we aspire, when one of them is so happy as to be married to a sage, while Elementaries of the masculine kind can attain to the same glorious end by effecting a union with the daughters of the human race."

This belief is responsible, of course, for the many fairy wives of fable. In the legends and folk-stories of nearly all countries, Asiatic and European, we find the enchanted-spouse motif occurring again and again, and some very curious parallels exist between such fables of the East and of the West ; so that the idea of the fairy wife would appear to be common to all peoples, or traceable to some parent legend of remote antiquity.

In the medieval French romance of *Mélusine*, the maiden of that name weds Raymond, on the condition that he shall never seek to see her upon a certain day in every week. To this he solemnly pledges himself. Eight sons are born of the union, and seven of these become great warriors. All goes well until the unhappy Raymond is persuaded, by the specious arguments of his brother, to break his solemn vow.

On the day of Mélusine's usual withdrawal from his society, he goes in search of her, and finds her in a bath, the lower part of her body having been transformed into that of a serpent ! When, later, in the course of a quarrel, Raymond unjustly reproaches Mélusine as " a false serpent," she, though against her will, takes flight through the open window in the likeness of a dragon.

This sufficiently remarkable fable becomes more remarkable still when considered side by side with " The Story of Hasan of El-Basrah " in *The Thousand and One Nights*. Hasan becomes enamoured of a damsel who " surpassed in her loveliness the beauties of the world, and the lustre of her face outshone the bright full moon ; she surpassed the branches in the beauty of her bending motions, and confounded the mind with apprehension of incurring calumny. . . . She had a mouth like the seal of Suleyman, and hair blacker than the night of estrangement is to the afflicted, distracted lover, and a forehead like the new moon of the Festival of Ramadan, and eyes resembling the eyes of the gazelles, and an aquiline nose brightly shining, and cheeks like anemones, and lips like coral, and teeth like pearls strung on necklaces of native gold, and a neck like molten silver, above a figure like a willow-branch."

This damsel was the daughter of one of the Kings of the *ginn*, and when, by means not over-scrupulous, he had secured her for his wife, Hasan, like Raymond, passed many years in happiness with her. Then, in her husband's absence, the daughter of the *ginn* is given access to a certain magical " dress of feathers," contrary to the solemn injunctions of Hasan.

In the Arabian story this incident takes the place of Raymond's intrusion upon the bath of Mélusine. For the fairy wife " took the dress and opened it, and took her child in her bosom . . . and became a bird. . . ." Having left a message that Hasan, if he desired to meet her again, should come to her " in the islands of Wak-Wak " (said to lie east of Borneo), " she flew away with her children and sought her country."

Perhaps one of the oldest myths of this class is the Hindu legend of Urvasi and Pururavas ; but there is another very ancient Hindu legend, wherein Bheki, the frog, is a beautiful maiden who consents to wed a King on the extraordinary condition that he shall never show her a drop of water. Being faint, on one occasion, she is said to have asked for water, and he thoughtlessly giving her some, she immediately disappeared.

Paracelsus seems to have been responsible for the

creation of the term " Undines " (the water Elementals). In Fouqué's romance upon the subject, Undine takes the knight of her choice down into a submarine palace, where she marries him, making him promise that he will never speak angrily to her when on, or near to, any water. Needless to say, he breaks his promise.

One of the most uncanny creatures of the human invention, the werewolf, may be included among fairy spouses ; and a belief in the existence of these was current in ancient and medieval times, and prevails to this day among many savage races, and even in out-of-the-way parts of France, Russia, and Bulgaria.

In a quotation by Halliwell from a Bodleian MS. we read that :

" Ther ben somme that eten . . . men, and eteth noon other . . . fro that tyme that thei be a-charmed with mannys . . . for rather thei wolde be deed . . . men shulde be war of hem."

Wlislocki, writing so recently as 1891, tells us of a gipsy fiddler's wife at Tórész, in the north of Hungary, about ten years earlier, who kept the family in mutton and enabled her husband to establish a profitable business as an innkeeper by her nocturnal expeditions in wolf's shape. The village priest cured the woman, we are informed, by sprinkling her and the house with holy water, and the peasants murdered the husband. At the time that Wlislocki wrote there were then living in the village, according to his account, two of the men who participated in the deed.[1]

Similar fables of semi-fairy unions, except that the husband is the supernatural partner, are the Græco-Roman myth of Cupid and Psyche and the Sicilian tale of the girl who wedded a green bird, which, on bathing in a pan of milk, became a handsome youth. But the favourite motif, which runs through the mythology of the East and West, while it cannot fairly be traced to any one source, is that of the fairy wife.

---

[1] So recently as the winter of 1913, a report reached me, from a British Tropical Colony, of a were-wolf. The circumstances were attested by several witnesses.

X. THE " CELESTIAL INTELLIGENCER "

One of the most remarkable works ever contributed to the literature of the occult is that called *The Magus*. I append the full title at the end of this chapter (p. 41).

In the section of this huge and elaborate work entitled " Natural Magic," the author says, " There are some *collyriums* which make us see the images of spirits in the air or elsewhere ; which I can make of the gall of a man and the eyes of a black cat, and some other things. The same is made, likewise, of the blood of a lapwing, bat and a goat ; and if a smooth, shining piece of steel be smeared over with the juice of mugwort, and be made to fume, it causes invocated spirits to appear."

Furthermore he tells us that in the colic, if a live duck be applied to the belly, it takes away the pain, and the duck dies. If one take the heart out of any animal, and, whilst it is warm, bind it to a patient suffering from a quartan fever, it drives it away. " So if any one shall swallow the heart of a lapwing, swallow, weasel, or a mole, while it is yet living and warm with natural heat, it improves his intellect, and helps him to remember, understand, and foretell things to come. Hence this general rule—that whatever things are taken for magical uses from animals, whether they are stone, members, hair, excrements, nails, or anything else, they must be taken from those animals while they are yet alive, and if it is possible, that they may live afterwards.

" If you take the tongue of a frog, you put the frog into water again : and Democritus writes, that if any one shall take out the tongue of a water-frog, no other part of the animal sticking to it, and lay it upon the place where the heart of a woman beats, she is compelled, against her will, to answer whatsoever you shall ask of her. Also, take the eyes of a frog, which must be extracted before sunrise, and bound to the sick party, and the frog to be let go again blind into the water, the party shall be cured of a tertian ague ; also, the same will, being bound with the flesh of a nightingale in the skin of a hart, keep a person always wakeful without sleeping.

" So the right eye of a serpent, being applied to the soreness of the eyes, cures the same, if the serpent be let go alive. So, likewise, the tooth of a mole, being taken out alive and afterwards let go, cures the toothache ; and dogs will never bark at those who have the tail of a weasel that has escaped. Democritus says, that if the tongue of the chameleon be taken alive, it conduces to good success in trials, and likewise to women in labour ; but it must be hung up on some part of the outside of the house ; otherwise, if brought into the house, it might be most dangerous.

" There are very many properties that remain after death ; and these are things in which the idea of the matter is less swallowed up in them ; even after death, that which is immortal in them will work some wonderful things : as in the skins we have mentioned of several wild beasts, which will corrode and eat one another after death ; also, the drum made of the rocket-fish drives away all creeping things at what distance soever the sound is heard ; and strings of an instrument made of the guts of a wolf, and being strained upon a harp or a lute, with strings made of sheep-guts, will make no harmony."

THE "CELESTIAL INTELLIGENCER"

THE
MAGUS
OR
CELESTIAL INTELLIGENCER

BEING

A Complete System of
OCCULT PHILOSOPHY

IN THREE BOOKS:
Containing the Ancient and Modern Practice of the Cabalistic Art,
Natural and Celestial Magic, &c; showing the wonderful Effects
that may be performed by a knowledge of the CELESTIAL
INFLUENCES, *the occult properties of metals, herbs and stones,*
and the
APPLICATION OF ACTIVE TO PASSIVE PRINCIPLES.
Exhibiting
THE SCIENCES OF NATURAL MAGIC;
Alchymy, or Hermetic Philosophy;
also
The NATURE, CREATION, AND FALL OF MAN;
His natural and supernatural Gifts; the magical Power inherent
in the Soul, &c.; with a great variety of rare Experiments in
Natural Magic:
THE CONSTELLATORY PRACTICE, or TALISMANIC MAGIC;
The Nature of the Elements, Stars, Planets, Signs, &c.;
The Construction and Composition of all Sorts of Magic Seals,
Images, Rings, Glasses, &c.:
The Virtue and Efficacy of Numbers, Characters, and
Figures, of good and evil spirits.
MAGNETISM,
And Cabalistical or Ceremonial Magic;
In which the secret Mystries of the Cabala are explained; the
operation of good and evil spirits; all kinds of Cabalistic
Figures, Tables, Seals, and Names, with their Use, &c. The
Times, Bond, Offices, and Conjuration of Spirits, to which
is added
*Biographia Antiqua, or the Lives of the most eminent Philosophers,
Magi, &c.*
The Whole Illustrated with a great Variety of
CURIOUS ENGRAVINGS, MAGICAL AND CABALISTICAL
FIGURES, &c.
By
FRANCIS BARRETT, F.R.C.
Professor of Chemistry, Natural and Occult Philosophy, the
Cabala, &c., &c.

LONDON
Printed for Lackington, Allen and Co., Temple of the Muses,
Finsbury Square.
1801.

XI. THE SHADOW ARMY

Book II, Part III of this huge and elaborately illustrated work (original copies of which are rare) deals with the " Particular Composition of the Magical Circle."

The following instructions, we learn, are the principle and sum-total of all that has gone before, only, says *The Magus :*

" We have brought it rather into a closer train of experiment and practice than any of the rest ; for here you may behold the distinct functions of the spirits ; likewise the whole perfection of magical ceremonies is here described, syllable by syllable."

But as the greatest power is attributed to the circles (" for they are certain fortresses "), I shall now give some particulars respecting the composition and figure of a circle.

The forms of circles are not always one and the same, but are changed according to the order of spirits that are to be called—their places, times, days, and hours ; for in making a circle it should be considered in what time of the year, what day, and what hour ; what spirits you would call, and to what star or region they belong, and what functions they have : therefore, to begin, let there be made three circles of the latitude of nine feet, distant one from another about a hand's breadth.

First, write in the middle circle the name of the hour wherein you essay the magical task ; in the second place, write the name of the angel of the hour ; in the third place, the seal of the angel of the hour ; fourthly, the name of the angel that rules the day, and the names of his ministers ; in the fifth place, the name of the present time ; sixthly, the names of the spirits ruling in that part of time, and their *presidents ;* seventhly, the name of the head of the sign ruling in the time ; eighthly, the name of the earth, according to the time of conjuration ; ninthly, and in order to complete the middle circle, write the name of the sun and moon, according to the said rule of the time : " for as the times are changed, so are the names."

In the outer circle let there be drawn, in the four angles,

" the names of the great presidential spirits of the air that day wherein you do this work, viz. the name of the king and his three ministers. Without the circle, in four angles, let *pentagons* be made. In the inner circle write four divine names, with four crosses interposed : in the middle of the circle, viz. towards the east, let be written Alpha ; towards the west, Omega ; and let a cross divide the middle of the circle."

When the circle is thus finished, according to rule, one must proceed to consecrate and bless it, in the following manner :

" In the name of the holy, blessed, and glorious Trinity, proceed we to our work in these mysteries to accomplish that which we desire ; we therefore, in the names aforesaid, consecrate this piece of ground for our defence, so that no spirit whatsoever shall be able to break these boundaries, neither be able to cause injury nor detriment to any of us here assembled ; but that they may be compelled to stand before the circle, and answer truly our demands, so far as it pleaseth Him who liveth for ever and ever ; and who says, I am Alpha and Omega, the Beginning and the End, which is, and which was, and which is to come, the Almighty ; I am the First and the Last, who am living and was dead ; and behold I live for ever and ever ; and I have the keys of death and hell. Bless, O Lord ! this creature of earth wherein we stand ; confirm, O God ! thy strength in us, so that neither the adversary nor any evil thing may cause us to fall, etc., etc. Amen."

The following particulars should also be studied :

Benediction of Perfumes

" The God of Abraham, God of Isaac, God of Jacob, bless here the creatures of these kinds, that they may fill up the power and virtue of their odours ; so that neither the enemy nor any false imagination may be able to enter into them ; etc. Then sprinkle the same with holy water."

The Exorcism of Fire into which the Perfumes are to be put

" I exorcise thee, O thou creature of fire, by the only true God Jehovah, Adonai, Tetragrammaton, that forthwith thou cast away every phantasm from thee, that it shall do no hurt to any one. We beseech thee, O Lord, to bless this creature of fire, and sanctify it so that it may be blessed to set forth the praise and glory of thy holy name, and that no hurt may be permitted to come to the exorciser or spectators ; etc. *Amen.*"

Of the Habit of the Exorcist

" It should be made of fine white linen and clean, and to come round the body loose, but close before and behind."

Of the Pentacle of Solomon (for the figure see Plate)

" It is always necessary to have this pentacle in readiness to bind with, in case the spirits should refuse to be obedient, as they can have no power over the exorcist while provided with and fortified by the pentacle, the virtue of the holy names therein written presiding with wonderful influence over the spirits.

" It should be made in the day and hour of Mercury upon parchment made of kidskin, or virgin, or pure, clean, white paper ; and the figures and letters wrote in pure gold ; and it ought to be consecrated and sprinkled (as before often spoken) with holy water."

When the vesture is put on, it will be convenient to say the following oration :

An Oration when the Habit or Vesture is put on

" Anoor, Amacor, Amides, Theodonias, Anitor ; by the merits of the angels, O Lord, I will put on the garment of salvation, that this which I desire I may bring to effect, through thee, the most holy Adonai, whose kingdom endureth for ever and ever. *Amen.*"

XII. THE MASSING OF THE SHADES

I have omitted many of the elaborate particulars which follow, firstly, in order that I may not weary you, and, secondly, because it forms no part of my intention to tempt the curious to dabble in a dangerous pursuit ; but the lengthy ceremonial being duly performed, we are assured that there will appear infinite visions, apparitions, phantasms, etc., beating of drums, and the sound of all kinds of musical instruments ; " which is done by the spirits, that with the terror they might force some of the companions out of the circle, because they can effect nothing against the exorcist himself : after this you shall see an infinite company of archers, with a great multitude of horrible beasts, which will arrange themselves as if they would devour the companions ; nevertheless fear nothing."

Thereupon, the exorcist, holding the pentacle in his hand, must say, "Avoid hence these iniquities, by virtue of the banner of God." At this, the spirits will be compelled to obey the exorcist, and the company shall see them no more.

Then let the exorcist, stretching out his hand with the pentacle, say :

" Behold the pentacle of *Solomon*, which I have brought into your presence ; behold the person of the exorcist in the middle of the exorcism, who is armed by God, without fear, and well provided, who potently invocateth and calleth you by exorcising ; come, therefore, with speed, by the virtue of these names, Aye Saraye, Aye Saraye ; defer not to come, by the eternal names of the living and true God, Eloy, Archima, Rabur, and by the pentacle of Solomon here present which powerfully reigns over you, and by the virtue of the celestial spirits, your lords ; and by the person of the exorcist, in the middle of the exorcism ; being conjured, make haste and come, and yield obedience to your master, who is called Octinomos."

This invocation being performed, immediately there will be hissings in the four parts of the world, whereupon the exorcist must say :

" Why stay you ? Wherefore do you delay ? What do you ? Prepare yourselves to be obedient to your master in the name of the Lord, Bathat or Vachat rushing upon Abrac, Abeor coming upon Aberer."

Then they will immediately come in their proper forms ; and :

" When you see them before the circle, show them the pentacle covered with fine linen ; uncover it, and say, ' Behold your confusion if you refuse to be obedient ' ; and suddenly they will appear in a peaceable form, and will say, ' Ask what you will, for we are prepared to fulfil all your commands, for the Lord hath subjected us hereunto.' "[1]

[1] There is a very fine account of a conjuration in Lytton's *A Strange Story*.

SORCERY AND SORCERERS

Their Familiar Forms are as follows :

The spirits appear generally of a great and full stature, soft and phlegmatic, of colour like a black, obscure cloud, having a swollen countenance, with eyes red and full of water, a bald head, and teeth like a wild boar ; their motion is like an exceeding great motion of the sea. For their sign there will appear an exceeding great rain, and their particular shapes are :

A King, like an archer, riding upon a doe.

A little boy.

A woman hunter with a bow and arrows.

A cow ; a little dog ; a goose.

A green or silver coloured garment.

An arrow ; a creature with many feet.

The spirits of the air of Friday are subject to the west wind ; their nature is to give silver, to incite men, and incline them to luxury, to cause marriages, to allure men to love women, to cause or take away infirmities, and to do all things which have motion.

Their Familiar Shapes

They appear with a fair body, of middle stature, with an amiable and pleasant countenance, of colour white or green, their upper parts golden ; the motion of them is like a clear star. For their sign will appear naked virgins round the circle, which will strive to allure the invocator to dalliance with them ; but :

Their Particular Shapes are

A King, with sceptre, riding on a camel.

A naked girl ; a she-goat.

A camel ; a dove.

A white or green garment.

Flowers ; the herb Savine.

But there are repulsive Elemental forms, as well, in addition to those mentioned by Barrett, having, for instance, the appearances of huge insects, with heads of birds or of human beings. A gruesome theory, employed finely in fiction by Sheridan le Fanu, has been advanced, according to which the creatures seen by sufferers from delirium tremens, by opium-smokers and by other drug-slaves, are simply forms taken by the lowest class of Elementals which the action of the poison has in some way rendered visible.[1]

I will transcribe here, in dismissing Francis Barrett, an interesting " advertisement " from *The Magus*:

Advertisement

The Author of this work respectfully informs those who are curious in the studies of Art and Nature, especially of Natural and Occult Philosophy, Chemistry, Astrology, etc., etc., that, having been indefatigable in his researches into those sublime sciences, of which he has treated at large in this book, that he gives private instructions and lectures upon any of the above mentioned sciences ; in the course of which he will discover many curious and rare experiments. Those who become students will be initiated into the choicest operations of Natural Philosophy, Natural Magic, the Cabala, Chemistry, the Talismanic Art, Hermetic Philosophy, Astrology, Physiognomy, etc., etc.   Likewise they will acquire the knowledge of the Rites, Mysteries, Ceremonies, *and* Principles *of the ancient Philosophers, Magi, Cabalists, Adepts, etc.   The purpose of this School (which will consist of no greater number than Twelve Students) being to investigate the hidden treasures of Nature ; to bring the mind to a contemplation of the* Eternal Wisdom ; *to promote the discovery of whatever may conduce to the perfection of Man ; the alleviating the miseries and calamities of this life, both in respect of ourselves and others ; the study of morality and religion here, in order to secure to ourselves felicity hereafter ; and finally the promulgation of whatever may conduce to the general happiness and welfare of mankind. Those who feel themselves thoroughly disposed to enter upon such a course of studies, as is above recited, with the same principles of philanthropy with which the Author invites the lovers of philosophy and wisdom to incorporate themselves in so select, permanent, and desirable a society, may speak with the Author upon the subject, at any time between the hours of Eleven and Two o'clock, at* 99, Norton Street, Mary-le-Bonne.   *Letters (post paid) upon any subject treated of in this Book will be duly answered, with the necessary information.*

[1] I had originally intended to include a *complete* ceremony of conjuration in the foregoing chapters, but it has been pointed out to me that this might be undesirable in a book of the present description.

CPSIA information can be obtained at www.ICGtesting.com
Printed in the USA
LVOW12s1828160314

377626LV00001B/33/P

Still Unbroken

A Woman's Truth About Love, Respect, and Choosing Herself

The lessons life taught me after the pain, after the heartbreak, and after the silence.

By
Tonia A Strickland